This book belongs to

_____

Today is _____

and this is the day of my Baptism.

My Baptism took place at

_____

_____

Officiating at my Baptism was

the Reverend_____

Introduction

Thank you for your interest in this, the first in a series of books from *Aunt Dee's Attic*. The series is intended to commemorate, record, and tell stories of the various special days and one-time events in our lives.

Appropriately, we think, this first book embraces one of the first special days and events a person generally experiences, that of *Baptism*.

This book is presented first and foremost as a source of entertainment, one that you will read to your baby or young child, and one that you and your child may enjoy reading and looking at for years to come.

Often in our busy lives, we forget what these special days and one-time events are all about. Therefore, in our books we take the liberty to expand on the background of certain events, their meaning, how they originated, and perhaps share some anecdotal experiences of others. For this book on *Baptism*, we include short essays on:

- Why We Baptize
- Why and How We Use Water in Baptism
- The Baptism of Jesus Christ
- How Jesus Conferred the Right to Baptize to the Apostles
- Anointing With Oil
- The Baptismal Gown

Finally, because *Baptism* is a joyous occasion, one of celebration that you and your baptismal child will want to remember always, we have provided a place to describe the events of the day and for the parents, godparents/sponsors, and others to record their thoughts and messages. This book also provides space to insert photographs and small souvenirs of the day. Please enjoy your book.

THIS IS A VERY SPECIAL DAY

A place of fascination and imagination, Mystery and intrigue

Family histories and heirlooms, Books, legends and leagues

Stories of love and compassion, Raymond's love letters to Aunt Nell

Special days with stories to tell

A Special Thank You to:

Kristin Bos and Jill Cooke for their inspiration and critique;

Todd, Kris, Lauren, and Drew Bos for their presence;

The Reverend Father Roger Prokop, Pastor of St. Thomas the Apostle
Catholic Church, Ann Arbor, Michigan, and

The Reverend Richard L. Dake, Pastor of Chelsea United Methodist Church,
Chelsea, Michigan, for their review and guidance;

Barbara M. Kelly for helping us to dot our "i's" and cross our "t's"; and

Nicholas James Scodeller for sharing his special day.

Nihil Obstat: Rev. Msgr. Sylvester I. Fedewa, S.T.L., D.Min.
Censor Librorum

Imprimatur: Most Reverend Carl F. Mengeling
Bishop of Lansing
November 9, 2004

A Book from Aunt Dee's Attic

Published by Aunt Dee's Attic, Inc.
415 Detroit Street, Suite 200
Ann Arbor, MI 48104

Printed and bound in Canada

Library of Congress Cataloging-in-Publication Data - application in progress
Summary: A story of an infant's baptism with short essays on
the sacrament of baptism, its origin and traditions.

ISBN 0-9679437-0-1

7 8 9 10 11 12 13 14 15

First Edition

www.auntdeesattic.com

Today I Was Baptized

Written by **Dianne Ahern**

Illustrated by **Katherine Larson**

I knew immediately

when I awoke this morning that today would be a special day. You see, my Mom was excited about something and during my bath we did a lot more "cooing" and "wooing" to each other than usual.

Already I have learned to tell from the tone of her voice what will be an ordinary day and what will be a special day.

In fact, the entire house
is filled with excitement.
Everybody is "getting ready"
for something...
SOMETHING SPECIAL.

On my dressing table I can see that in place of
my comfy play clothes hangs the most beautiful
white gown I have ever seen. "Is that for me!?"
I want to shout.

Sure enough, as soon as everyone else
has on their dress-up clothes,
Mom and Dad begin
putting the beautiful
white gown on me.

I squirm and giggle
and wiggle. Mom
and Dad tug and hug.
There, it is finally on me.

WOW, I look like an angel!

We all get in the car and off we go to a place called "church."

The church is big, with more people inside than I have ever seen. The light coming through the windows puts rainbows on the faces and places.

Up in front, there is a big man. "Look!"
He has on a white gown and colorful scarf.
His gown is almost as beautiful as mine.

The big man in
the white gown
smiles at me
and touches
my cheek.

This is going
to be OK!

"What do you
want for this child today?" The big man loudly,
proudly asks my Mom and Dad.

"Baptism," they reply.

"Are there sponsors or godparents?" he asks.

"**I** am the godmother," says the woman standing beside my Mom. Mom places me in her arms. "I am the godfather," says the man standing next to her.

The big man in the white gown asks my parents and godparents if they will love and guide me, help me to live a Christian life, to accept God's grace, and to resist and reject evil powers.

They say they will.

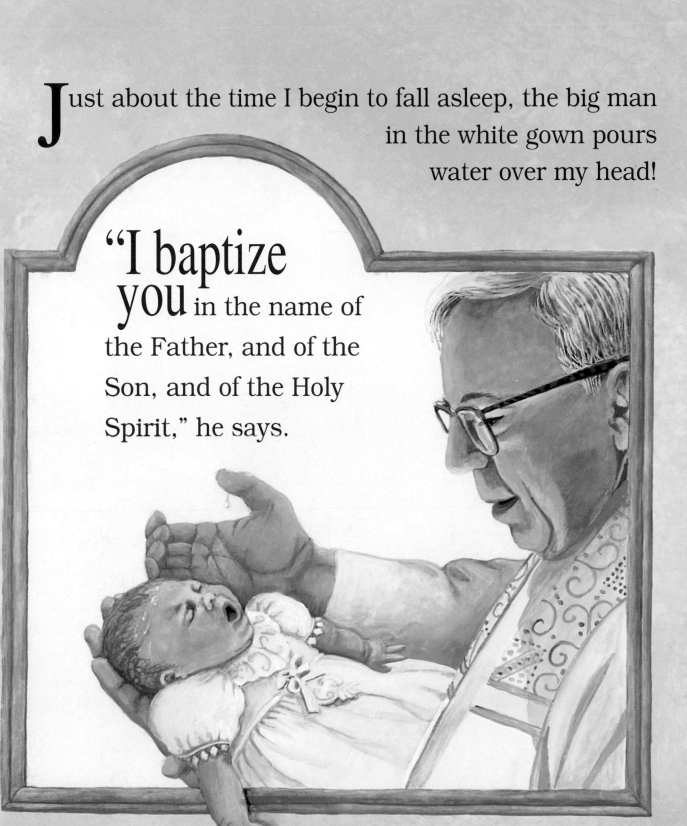

Just about the time I begin to fall asleep, the big man in the white gown pours water over my head!

"I baptize you in the name of the Father, and of the Son, and of the Holy Spirit," he says.

I make a funny face. This must be amusing because everybody smiles and giggles while I squirm and wiggle.

The big man in the white gown turns to the people in the church and says, "Please welcome this new Christian and the newest member of our Church."

The people cheer and clap their hands. This is SPECIAL.

We all go home and there is a big celebration. There is food and music, presents and lively conversation.

What a wonderful and

Special Day!

My Mom and I go to my room where it is quiet. I could use a little nap. This has been a very busy day.

Mom and I sit in her rocking chair and she talks to me in her special voice. "My precious little one," she says. "Today we helped you to become a Christian. You received God's grace through Baptism. From now on, God's grace and our love will help you to grow strong in faith and spirit."

As I drift off to sleep, I feel the flutter of little angel wings inside my soul.

You see, today was a very special day.
Today, I was baptized.

Short Essays on Baptism

Why We Baptize

Baptism is the sacrament of initiation and incorporation into the Body of Christ. Through Baptism, children born into the brokenness of the world receive the cleansing and renewing forgiveness of God, are recipients of His grace and love, become members of His Church, and receive an indelible mark necessary for salvation.

Most Christians believe there is a "spiritual disease" we all get just by being born into a world that is out-of-kilter. (We know the world is out-of-kilter because there are wars, family squabbles, and sometimes problems we have to deal with that we ourselves have not caused.) We call that spiritual disease, Original Sin.

In the beginning, after God made heaven and earth and all the animals, God made man and woman in his likeness. He gave them the most beautiful place to live. The man and woman were named Adam and Eve, and their home was called the Garden of Eden. God gave them something special, something He did not give to the plants and animals. He gave them the ability to speak, to think, and to make decisions. God trusted they would use this special ability to live rich and fruitful lives, to do good deeds, and to repel the powers of Satan.

God told Adam and Eve that they could have and do anything they wanted, except He forbid them to eat the fruit of one special tree. Then along came Satan in the form of a serpent. The serpent encouraged Adam and Eve to eat the fruit of the forbidden tree. After all, what harm could it do?

Adam, having the God given ability to determine right from wrong, decided to follow the serpent's temptation anyway. When Adam thought God wasn't looking, he took and ate the forbidden fruit. This was against God's command; Adam knew it, but he did it anyway.

God did see Adam eat the forbidden fruit, and shamed him, saying, "You have sinned, not just for yourself, but for all of mankind." This spoiled it for the rest of us, because, being descendants of Adam, we all inherited part of his sin, the Original Sin.

In His mercy, though, God gave us the Sacrament of Baptism to be used as an inoculation against the ravages of the spiritual disease called Original Sin. Baptism frees us of Original Sin *and* provides us with the grace of God and the strength of His Church to live rich and fruitful lives. However, as with Adam and Eve, how we *decide* to live our lives is up to us.

We should note that the word Adam, in the Hebrew language, means "man" or "humankind." The Genesis story may not only be an account of how the world got out-of-kilter; it may also be a biography of you and me.

Why and How We Use Water In Baptism

Throughout all time, water has been characterized as being the source of life and fruitfulness, a source of death and destruction, and has the ability to cleanse and refresh.

- Water from hurricanes and floods destroy life and property

- Without water, rivers run dry and the fertile earth becomes desert

- Water that falls on the earth brings forth new foliage

- Water brings health and life to those who drink it

God's use of water is referenced in baptismal prayers:

> *When nothing existed but chaos, you swept across the dark waters and brought forth light.*

> *In the days of Noah you saved those on the ark through water. After the flood you set in the clouds a rainbow.*

> *When you saw your people as slaves in Egypt, you led them to freedom through the sea. Their children you brought through the River Jordan to the land which you promised.*

> *In the fullness of time you sent Jesus, nurtured in the water of a womb*

In Baptism, water is administered three times as the priest/minister recites the words, "*N.,* I baptize you in the Name of the Father, and of the Son, and of the Holy Spirit."

First, water is administered to destroy or drown the sin that each of us is born with or has committed between the time of birth and baptism. The water then cleanses and purifies the soul. With the final administration of water the person is reborn and becomes a member of the Church, the mystical body of Christ. Through the Sacrament of Baptism, the person enters the Kingdom of God. He is saved.

Many Christian faiths perform baptism by pouring or sprinkling water over the head of the baptismal participant. Others practice baptism by immersion.

The practice of immersion reflects the manner in which Christ was baptized. In this form of baptism, the first immersion or plunge in water symbolizes death of the sinful man. The baptized person on successive immersions is then reborn and becomes a member of the Church.

The Baptism of Jesus Christ

Did you know that Jesus Christ was baptized even though he was born without sin?

As Jesus approached adulthood and was about to go out into the world to begin his earthly ministry, he asked John the Baptist, who was one of His disciples, to baptize Him.

The baptismal rites that John was performing at the time were for repentance from and forgiveness of sin in preparation for the coming of the Kingdom of God. John was calling on people to confess and turn from their sins, and to show the fruit of their repentance by submitting to baptism. Baptism therefore was an outward sign of an inward work, one performed in anticipation of the coming of the Messiah.

That Jesus would ask to be baptized was surprising to John because he knew Jesus to be the Son of God, the true Messiah, and without sin.

When Jesus approached John, however, He made it clear that His baptism was not for the repentance of sin, but as an act of obedience to the Father. God said people must be baptized and Jesus followed His rules. Jesus was deliberately and consciously establishing a standard of behavior and setting an example for His disciples and others to follow.

Once Jesus was baptized, and as He came up from the water of the River Jordan, the heavens opened to Him and He saw the Spirit of God descending like a dove and alighting on him. A voice from heaven said, "This is my Son, the Beloved, with whom I am well pleased." *(Matthew 3:13)*

NOTE: The baptism for repentance of sin that John performed is different than the Christian baptism performed after Christ's death and resurrection. The Christian baptism is for the "washing" away of sin, not the repentance of sin. Christian baptism is a figure of death, burial, and resurrection of Christ and our being raised with Him.

How Jesus Conferred the Right to Baptize to the Apostles

Jesus Christ instituted the Sacrament of Baptism through the Apostles. He not only commanded His Disciples to baptize and gave them the form to be used, but He also declared the absolute necessity of Baptism.

> *"Unless a man be born again of water and the Holy Spirit, he can not enter into the Kingdom of God." (John 3)*

> *During His ministry on earth, Jesus authorized His disciples to baptize. (John 4:1,2)*

> *Jesus said to his disciples, "Go into all the world and preach the gospel to the whole creation. He who believes and is baptized will be saved; but he who does not believe will be condemned." (Mark, 16:15-16)*

> *When He was ready to ascend into heaven after His resurrection, His last command was "Go ye therefore, and teach all nations, baptizing them in the name of the Father, and of the Son, and of the Holy Spirit." (Matthew 28:19)*

Today, bishops, priests, deacons, and local pastors are the ministers of Baptism. The rite, passed down through the Apostles, is performed on both infants and adults, but it need be performed only once.

Under extraordinary conditions, when a person is in an emergency situation, is near death, and has not been baptized, baptism can be administered validly by any person who observes the essential conditions. The belief is that the unbaptized person should receive the Grace of God, have sins forgiven, and have the opportunity to enter the Kingdom of God. The person recognizing the emergency and fully comprehending the need and responsibility for baptism must pour water upon the one to be baptized and, at the same time, pronounce the words: "I baptize you in the name of the Father, and of the Son, and of the Holy Spirit."

Anointing With Oil

Some religions, most notably Catholic, anoint the infant/person with sacred chrism, perfumed oil, during the baptism ceremony. This signifies the gift of the Holy Spirit to the newly baptized, who has become a Christian, that is, one "anointed" by the Holy Spirit, incorporated into Christ who is the anointed priest, prophet, and king.

Christ means the "anointed" one. The infant/person following baptism is anointed and becomes "Christ-ed" or Christian.

The Baptismal Gown

The white vestment worn for baptism reflects the purity of the soul following Baptism and that the person has risen with Christ.

The baptismal gown selection and preparation has become a special ritual in itself. Many families pass the baptismal gown down through the generations. Others select a new gown for each child's baptism.

My Baptism Memories

The Baptismal gown I wore today is: *(describe)*

_____
_____
_____
_____

My parents had a celebration following my Baptism, and it included:
(describe the celebration, what foods were served, special decorations and favors, unusual events of the day, etc.)

_____
_____
_____
_____
_____
_____
_____
_____

The people who helped me to celebrate my baptism include:

_____
_____
_____
_____
_____
_____
_____
_____
_____
_____
_____

My Baptism Memories

Gifts I received today include:

_____

_____

_____

_____

_____

_____

_____

A Message from Mom on the day of my Baptism:

_____

_____

_____

_____

_____

_____

_____

_____

A Message from Dad on the day of my Baptism:

_____

_____

_____

_____

_____

_____

_____

My Baptism Memories

Messages from my Godparents, Sponsors, and other friends on the day of my Baptism:

_____
_____
_____
_____
_____
_____
_____
_____
_____
_____
_____
_____

Photographs and Other Memories

Photographs and Other Memories